I0762650

Little Mitchie

UNDER THE SEA EATS

RECIPES FROM THE OCEAN

KIDS IN THE KITCHEN

Joanne Mattern

CREATING YOUNG NONFICTION READERS

Little Mitchie books spark curiosity and support early nonfiction reading for students in Grades 2-3. Designed to build vocabulary, support second language learners, and prepare readers for middle-grade content, each book includes helpful tips for parents and educators to build confidence and deepen understanding of the world.

TIPS FOR READING NONFICTION WITH BEGINNING READERS

Talk about Nonfiction

Begin by explaining that nonfiction books give us information that is true. The book will be organized around a specific topic or idea, and we may learn new facts through reading.

Look at the Parts

Most nonfiction books have helpful features. Our *Little Mitchie* titles include color photographs and graphic aids, a table of contents, a glossary, and an index. Share the purpose of these features with your reader.

Color Photos and Graphic Aids

A lot of information can be found by "reading" photos, charts, maps, and other graphic aids found within nonfiction texts. Help your reader learn more about the different ways information can be displayed.

Table of Contents

Located at the front of the book, this list shows the big ideas within the text and the page numbers where they can be found.

Glossary

Located at the back of the book, the glossary defines key words and phrases that are related to the topic. These words and phrases can be found in the text in colored type.

Index

Located at the back of the book, an index is an alphabetical list of topics and the page numbers where they can be found.

With a little help and guidance about reading nonfiction, you can feel good about introducing a young reader to the world of *Little Mitchie* nonfiction books.

Little Mitchie is an imprint of:

2001 SW 31st Avenue
Hallandale, FL 33009
mitchelllanepub.com

First Edition, 2027.

Author: Joanne Mattern
Designer: Bobbie Houser
Editor: Madison Greve

Library of Congress Cataloging-in-Publication Data
Title: Under the Sea Eats: Recipes from the OceanFun / by Joanne Mattern

Description: Hallandale, FL : Mitchell Lane Publishers, [2027]

Identifiers:
ISBN 979-8-89260-931-9 (library bound)
ISBN 979-8-90145-017-8 (eBook)

Library of Congress Control Number: 2026936390

PHOTO CREDITS
Alamy: GL Archive, 17; Shutterstock: Elena Shashkina, cover, 1, 19; Taras Grebinets, 4; Viktoriia Ablohina, 5; MissRissa, 7; WonderKimber, 9; Lika Mostova, 11; Sabbir Media, 13; Arina P Habich, 15; Brent Hofacker, 17; AtlasStudio, 21.

TABLE OF CONTENTS

HOW TO USE THIS BOOK

The kitchen is a great place to have fun! This book will help you make some delicious recipes.

Read each recipe first. Be sure to have everything you need in place before you start. Check that no one is **allergic** to any of the ingredients.

Wash your hands before you start.

Have an adult close by. Let them use knives and the stove.

Now, get ready to cook up some fun!

CONVERSION CHART

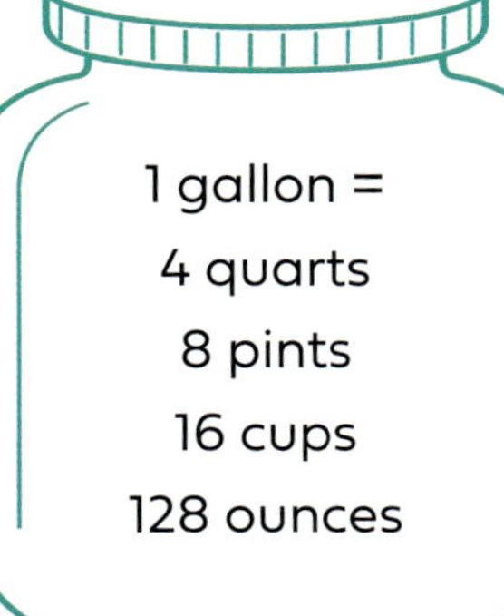

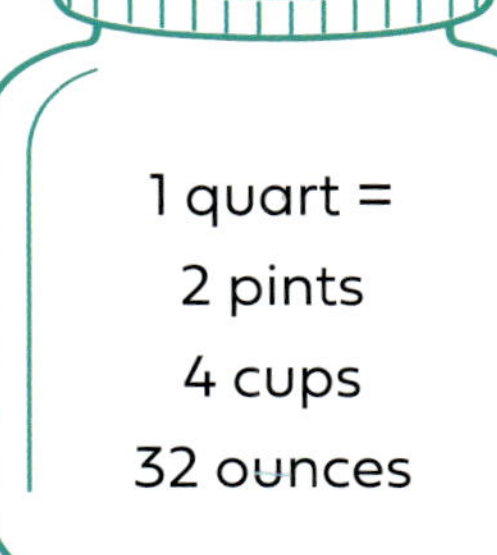

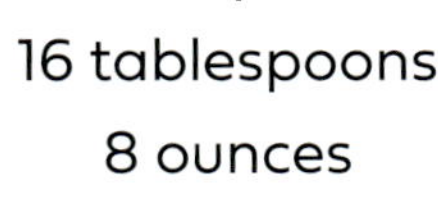

1 cup =
16 tablespoons
8 ounces

¾ cup =
12 tablespoons
6 ounces

½ cup =
8 tablespoons
4 ounces

⅓ cup =
5⅓ tablespoons
2⅔ ounces

¼ cup =
4 tablespoons
2 ounces

3 teaspoons = 1 tablespoon (½ ounce)
2 tablespoons = ⅛ cup (1 ounce)
4 tablespoons = ¼ cup (2 ounces)
5⅓ tablespoons = ⅓ cup (2⅔ ounces)
8 tablespoons = ½ cup (4 ounces)
12 tablespoons = ¾ cup (6 ounces)
32 tablespoons = 2 cups (16 ounces)

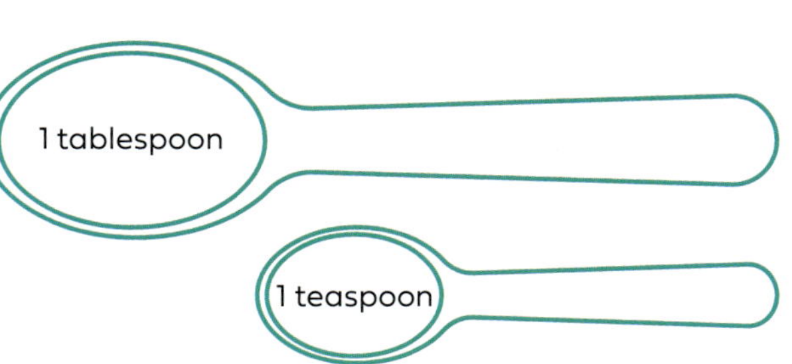

Chapter 1

SHARKS IN THE WATER CUPS

Janetta was having fun playing with her sister at the beach. Little Diana loved to run into the waves. She also loved to squeeze her toes in the sand.

"Diana, Mom made a special treat for us," Janetta said. She pulled some cups out of the bag their mother had packed. "These cups look just like the ocean. But there are sharks in the water!"

Diana laughed. "I like these sharks. They are fun to eat. But I hope we don't see any in the water for real!"

You will need:

Vanilla yogurt

Blue food coloring

1 container of Cool Whip™

1 cupcake pan

1 package of gummy shark candies

1 package of blue cupcake liners

¼-cup colorful sprinkles

Directions:

Place 1 cupcake liner into each cup in the cupcake pan.

Spoon yogurt into each cup.

Add a drop of blue food coloring to each cup. Stir until the yogurt turns blue.

Spoon Cool Whip™ on top of each cup of yogurt. This is the **seafoam**.

Place a candy shark on top of each cup.

Add a few sprinkles around each shark. These are the fish.

FUN FOOD FACT!
Gummy bears were first invented in Germany more than 100 years ago. Today, these snacks come in many different shapes!

Chapter 2

CRABBY APPLE FRUIT SALAD

Jorge was hungry when he came home from school. His mother took out a bag of apple slices for him. "What did you learn in school today?" she asked.

"We learned about ocean animals," Jorge said. "The **hermit crab** was my favorite. I'll bet I can make some crabs out of these apple slices."

"How can you do that?" his mother asked.

Jorge got out a few more ingredients. "Just watch," he said.

You will need:

1 apple

4 blueberries

1 strawberry

1 banana

1 package of candy eyes

Directions:

Have an adult slice the apple and strawberries in half. Set one half of the apple on a plate with the flat side down.

Have an adult cut the other half of the apple into small, thin slices. Place three slices on each side of the apple half to make the crab's legs.

Above the legs on each side of the apple, line up two blueberries so they stick out of the crab, like arms.

Top each arm with one strawberry half, flat side down, to make the claws.

Have an adult cut two thin slices of banana and place them on the plate, just above the apple half. Top each slice with a candy eyeball to make the crab's eyes.

FUN FOOD FACT!
China grows more apple trees than any other country.

Chapter 3

NO-BAKE SEASIDE S'MORES

"Are you ready to go to the beach?" Selena asked her brother, Ben.

"I can't wait," said Ben. "But I'm hungry."

"Let's pack a snack before we go," their father said. "I made something special for our day by the sea."

Selena and Ben laughed when they saw their snack. "These s'mores will get us in the mood to catch some waves!"

You will need:

8 graham crackers

4 bars of blue decorating chocolate

1 jar of marshmallow spread

1 package of candy pearls

Directions:

Carefully snap a graham cracker in half.

Have an adult cut or break a chocolate bar into a piece that will fit on top of the graham cracker half. You can lay the graham cracker half on top of the chocolate bar first to count how many squares will fit.

Add a small amount of marshmallow spread onto the graham cracker and stick the chocolate piece on top. Repeat these steps until you have a plate of chocolate grahams.

Scoop out some more marshmallow spread and slowly **drizzle** over the plate to look like seafoam.

Stick a few candy pearls around the marshmallow spread to make bubbles.

FUN FOOD FACT!
Graham crackers are named after Sylvester Graham. He invented them as a health food in 1829.

Chapter 4

Fruity Fish PB&Js

"How was your class trip to the **aquarium**?" Jade's mother asked.

"It was great!" Jade said. "I loved seeing so many different fish. They were swimming in big tanks." She sat down at the kitchen table. "May I have a snack, please?"

"Of course," her mother said. "I think you will like these special sandwiches. They will make you think of the fish you saw today!"

You will need:

1 **pita**

1 apple

1 banana

2 blueberries

½ cup Cheerios™

½-cup jelly (grape or strawberry—your choice!)

½-cup peanut butter

Directions:

Ask an adult to cut the pita into 4 equal pieces. Spread peanut butter and jelly inside 2 of the pita slices and lay on a plate to make the fishes' bodies.

Ask an adult to **core** the apple and cut the banana into thin, round slices.

Set 1 banana slice on each pita. Top each slice with a blueberry to make the fishes' eyes.

Place 1 apple slice above and below each eye to make the fins. Place 1 apple slice on the end of each pita to make the tails.

Add some Cheerios™ around the plate to make bubbles.

Pita bread has only 4 ingredients: flour, water, yeast, and salt.

GLOSSARY

allergic (uh-LER-jik)—having a bad reaction to a food

aquarium (uh-KWARE-ee-um)—a building or tank where people can see fish and other water animals

core (KOR)—to take out the seeds and middle part of an apple

drizzle (DRIZ-uhl)—to pour slowly with a small, light stream of liquid

hermit crab (HER-mit krab)—a type of ocean crab that lives inside of empty shells

pita (PEE-tah)—a kind of bread that has a pocket in the middle

seafoam (SEE-fohm)—bubbles that form on top of ocean waves

yeast (YEEST)—an ingredient that makes bread rise

FURTHER READING

Wilkes, Angela. *Children's Quick & Easy Cookbook*. DK Publishing, 2023.

Wood, Cathryn. *Adorable Animal Bakes*. Page Street Publishing, 2025.

ON THE INTERNET

"55 Fun Ocean Themed Party Food Ideas." UnexpectedlyDomestic.com
https://www.unexpectedlydomestic.com/ocean-themed-party-food/
From clever sandwiches to beautiful cupcakes, kids and adults alike will enjoy these ocean-themed recipes.

"Fun Ocean-Themed Snacks for Kids." I'm the Chef Too.com.
https://www.imthecheftoo.com/blogs/cooking-with-kids/fun-ocean-themed-snacks-for-kids?srsltid=AfmBOop9iwcM9CKBT0hU9Pzhxi4vgNrk2Cj47eqzjS1yBLJIqLm9-MSa
Children and adults will find many fun, ocean-themed recipes and learning ideas in this article.

INDEX

ABOUT THE AUTHOR

Joanne Mattern loves snacking and eating fun food! She has written many nonfiction books for children, including cookbooks and books about holidays. Joanne lives in New York State with her family.